Managed Detection and Response (MDR) Services

A Stakeholders Guide
By
Stephen M. Dye

Copyright © 2024 by Stephen M. Dye

Independently Published, Boca Raton, Florida, USA.
ISBN: 9798323689392
First Edition
Printed in the United States of America
Title: Managed Detection and Response (MDR) Services- a Stakeholders Guide by Stephen M. Dye
Identifiers: ISBN: 9798323689392
Subject/Topic: Managed Detection and Response (MDR) | Cybersecurity.

About the Author: See back cover.

Stephen M. Dye

DEDICATION:
This book is dedicated to my Loving parents:
Patricia Dye 1932-2014
and
Trevor Robert Dye 1933-2021

1   Contents

1 Purpose of this Book

This book aims to guide IT professionals and business executives through the complexities of selecting and implementing Managed Detection and Response (MDR) services. By demystifying MDR and detailing practical steps for evaluation and integration, readers will be equipped to make informed decisions that enhance their organization's cybersecurity posture.

1.1 Author's Background

Stephen M. Dye is the principal of UpLift Cyber, a company dedicated to startup, small and medium-sized businesses in need of developing or improving their Cyber Security Program. Stephen is an accomplished Cyber Security Professional with extensive experience in designing and implementing security infrastructures for diverse sectors and companies to include NTT DATA Federal, Virgin Voyages, Lattice and CRISPR. He holds a bachelor's degree in Electrical and Electronic Engineering from Bromley College of Technology, along with a slate of prestigious certifications including C|EH, CompTIA Security+, ITIL V3, IC Agile, and Scrum Manager. Stephen's expertise is augmented by executive education from Cornell's Johnson School of Business and an Honor Code Certificate in Cyber Security from MIT. As a published author, he has contributed significantly to the field with works such as "Secure Agile-25 Security user stories for agile developers", "Pragmatic Software Security", End-to End M2M and various books on GPS.

Contact Stephen at info@upliftcyber.com

2 Cybersecurity & the Evolution of MDR

2.1 Cybersecurity and how MDRs play a role.

Cybersecurity encompasses the practices, technologies, and processes designed to protect computers, networks, programs, and data from attack, damage, or unauthorized access. Its importance has grown in tandem with the global reliance on digital systems across all facets of life, from personal data storage to critical national infrastructure.

The history of cybersecurity dates back to the early days of computing, when the threats were mostly academic or experimental. However, the rise of the internet in the 1990s and the subsequent explosion in online activity led to an increase in digital vulnerabilities. As the world became more interconnected, the potential for cyber threats grew, prompting the development of sophisticated cybersecurity measures. The term "cybersecurity" itself began to gain currency in the early 2000s, as governments, businesses, and individuals grappled with the new reality of constant digital threats.

The need for cybersecurity has never been more apparent, highlighted by numerous high-profile breaches that have had significant economic, privacy, and security repercussions. For instance, the Equifax breach in 2017, which exposed the sensitive information of approximately 147 million people, could have been mitigated by implementing stringent security patches and following robust cybersecurity protocols. Similarly, the WannaCry ransomware attack in 2017 affected over 200,000 computers across 150 countries, exploiting vulnerabilities in outdated Windows systems that had not been updated with the latest security patches.

Another notable example is the 2013 Target data breach, where hackers accessed the credit card details of approximately forty million customers. This breach was primarily due to insufficient network segmentation and lax security standards. Adequate cybersecurity measures, such as comprehensive monitoring systems, regular security audits, and stringent access controls, could have significantly reduced the impact of these breaches.

Fast forward to recent times, below are some 2024 attacks and where an MDR was involved or could have been involved.

Microsoft Azure and Executive Accounts Breach (February 2024): This breach involved sophisticated phishing and cloud account takeovers targeting Microsoft 365 and Office Home applications. Key vulnerabilities were exploited, including a zero-day exploit in Microsoft Exchange servers. The breach affected hundreds of senior executive accounts and highlighted the need for robust cloud security measures and the potential benefit of an MDR service for continuous monitoring and response to such sophisticated threats.

Bank of America Data Breach (February 2024): This breach was traced to a cyberattack on Infosys McCamish Systems, affecting customer names, social security numbers, and account details. This incident underlines the importance of securing and monitoring third-party vendors, a task where MDR services could play a crucial role in detecting and mitigating such breaches.

"Mother of All Breaches" (MOAB): This massive breach involved the compilation of data from multiple previous breaches affecting platforms like LinkedIn, Twitter, Weibo, and Dropbox, among others. This breach underscores the need for robust cybersecurity measures and continuous monitoring, which MDR can provide, especially in identifying and responding to such large-scale data compilations before they become catastrophic.

Ransomware Attacks: Numerous ransomware attacks were reported, including significant incidents affecting Lurie Children's Hospital, California Union SEIU 1000, Hyundai Motor Europe, and several others. These attacks often caused severe operational disruptions. MDR services could significantly aid in early detection and isolation of ransomware threats, potentially preventing them from causing widespread damage.

Emerging Threats and Cloud Vulnerabilities: The rise in cloud intrusions and identity-based attacks, including the abuse of generative AI for social engineering, highlights the evolving nature of cyber threats. MDR services are vital in this context as they provide adaptive, real-time threat hunting and response capabilities that can evolve with and respond to modern cyber threats.

In summary, the recent breaches demonstrate the critical need for comprehensive cybersecurity strategies, including the deployment of MDR services. MDR can provide continuous monitoring, threat detection, and rapid response capabilities that are essential to defend against sophisticated and evolving cyber threats. These incidents underline the critical importance of cybersecurity in safeguarding sensitive information and maintaining the integrity of computing assets. As cyber threats continue to evolve in complexity and scale, the field of cybersecurity must adapt with advanced defensive technologies and proactive threat detection strategies to stay ahead of potential risks. This ongoing battle against cyber threats is not just about protecting data but is fundamental to maintaining trust in digital systems that power our modern world.

3 Rise of the MDR

In today's environment, where data breaches can result in substantial financial losses and damage to an organization's reputation, the need for more preventative and proactive cyber security measures is needed. Organizations are typically understaffed and not fully equipped as they should be to not only detect security events and alerts, but also act on them, taking proactive measures that would typically escalate. The role of MDR has become increasingly critical as a result. MDR services play a vital role in protecting digital assets, ensuring compliance with regulatory requirements, and maintaining business continuity. By providing 24/7 monitoring and expert analysis, MDR services help organizations to stay one step ahead of attackers. This is crucial not only for detecting and responding to attacks but also for planning and implementing effective defensive strategies that adapt to new threats as they emerge.

Moreover, MDR services are instrumental in ensuring compliance with various international and industry-specific standards, such as GDPR, HIPAA, and PCI DSS. These regulations require businesses to implement stringent data protection measures and to respond swiftly and effectively to security breaches. MDR providers, with their expertise and advanced technological capabilities, are uniquely equipped to help organizations meet these requirements.

MDRs have become a cornerstone of modern cybersecurity strategies, offering businesses the dynamic, proactive defense mechanisms necessary to navigate the complexities of the current threat landscape and safeguard their critical assets against potential cyber threats. This strategic importance underscores not just the functionality of MDR in threat mitigation but also its role in ensuring operational resilience and regulatory compliance.

3.1 Key Functions and Benefits of MDRs

As cyber threats become increasingly sophisticated, the need for robust cybersecurity strategies becomes paramount. MDR services represent a proactive approach to security that integrates technology, processes, and human expertise. This chapter delves into the core functions and benefits of MDR services, illustrating why they are essential for modern businesses.

3.1.1 Core Functions of MDR Services

MDR services provide comprehensive security solutions that go beyond traditional measures. The key functions and facets are discussed below and should be raised as talking points when engaging with a prospective vendor.

24/7 Monitoring and Alerting: MDR services ensure continuous monitoring of an organization's networks to detect any suspicious activity. This round-the-clock surveillance is crucial for early detection of potential threats, minimizing the window of opportunity for attackers.

Threat Detection: Utilizing advanced analytics and machine learning, MDR providers can identify threats with greater accuracy. This includes detecting malware, ransomware, and even insider threats by analyzing patterns and anomalies that may go unnoticed by traditional systems.

Incident Response: Once a threat is detected, MDR services act swiftly to contain the incident and mitigate damage. This response might include isolating affected systems, removing malicious files, or blocking malicious actors' access.

Risk Assessment and Management: MDR providers should conduct regular assessments to identify vulnerabilities within an organization's IT infrastructure. This proactive measure helps in prioritizing risks based on their potential impact and developing strategies to mitigate them effectively.

Expertise and Advanced Technology: MDR services provide access to top-tier security experts and state-of-the-art technologies that many organizations may not possess in-house. This expertise is crucial for understanding and mitigating complex cyber threats.

Cost-Effectiveness: By outsourcing to MDR providers, organizations can avoid the excessive costs associated with recruiting, training, and maintaining an in-house cybersecurity team. MDR services offer a scalable solution that can be adjusted as an organization grows. Consider that at least two people will be required in an organization to provide 24/7/365 coverage. This is for even the smallest organization. With two internal resources who will be required to understand what alerts and cyber events mean, experienced engineers will be required. This translates to the cost of employment, which will also include salary, benefits, shift allowances and training. MDR service providers will already have the trained, qualified staff available in their organization, also assigned to other customers who, through economic scaling will cost the end customer less.

Enhanced Compliance: MDR providers help organizations comply with various regulatory requirements by ensuring that their security measures are up to date with current laws and standards.

Strategic Security Insights: With continuous monitoring and data collection, MDR services provide valuable insights into security trends and threat landscapes. This information helps organizations in making informed decisions about their security policies and strategies.

Lower Insurance Premiums: The integration of MDR services into an organization's cybersecurity strategy offers a dynamic shield against cyber threats. With their comprehensive coverage, advanced technology, and cost-effective solutions, MDR services are thus highly effective breach mitigators. Cyber insurance premiums will be a lot lower than without employing an MDR service. This must be considered when weighing the costs: please consider the reduced premiums as an MDR cost mitigator.

3.1.2 Comparison with Traditional Methods

Whether using an MDR or in-house services, there will be costs involved in implementing the solution. There is also a cost to not implementing such a solution in the event of a breach. However, let us try to further justify procuring an MDR solution by comparing MDRs to traditional methods. MDR services offer a modern approach to cybersecurity, distinct from traditional security measures like firewalls, antivirus software, and intrusion detection systems (IDS). Below is a comparison highlighting how MDR improves efficiency, response times, and the utilization of threat intelligence:

3.1.3 Proactive Monitoring and Response

Traditional Methods: Traditional security tools often rely on predefined rules or signatures to detect threats. This approach can be effective against known threats but may fail to catch new, sophisticated attacks that do not match existing signatures.

MDR Services: MDR provides continuous monitoring and real-time analysis of security alerts. This approach uses advanced analytics, machine learning, and human expertise to identify and respond to anomalies that traditional tools and methods might miss, thus offering proactive threat hunting and incident response capabilities.

3.1.4 Threat Intelligence Utilization

Traditional Methods: While traditional methods do use threat intelligence, they often do so in a static way, applying updates periodically and relying heavily on known threat databases.

MDR Services: MDR integrates innovative threat intelligence in real-time, continuously updating its understanding of the threat landscape. This dynamic utilization helps in anticipating and defending against emerging threats more effectively, thereby enhancing predictive security postures.

3.1.5 Response Times

Traditional Methods: The response to threats can be slower, as it often requires manual intervention to update defenses or remediate after an attack is detected. There can be significant delays between the identification of a new threat and the deployment of effective countermeasures.

MDR Services: MDR services significantly improve response times by automating aspects of the detection, investigation, and response processes. MDR teams can isolate threats and initiate remedial actions in near real-time, minimizing the potential damage caused by breaches.

3.1.6 Scalability and Expertise

Traditional Methods: Scaling traditional security measures often requires substantial investment in both hardware and skilled personnel. The effectiveness of these measures is limited by the resources available for managing and updating the systems.

MDR Services: With MDR, organizations gain access to a team of security experts without the need for extensive internal expertise. This service is scalable and can adjust more fluidly to the organization's size and risk profile, providing cost-effective access to high-level security operations.

3.1.7 Integration and Automation

Traditional Methods: Integration between different traditional security tools can be challenging, often resulting in siloed systems that hinder efficient threat detection and response.

MDR Services: MDR solutions are typically designed to integrate seamlessly with existing IT environments, utilizing automation to streamline workflows and reduce the burden on internal teams. This integration allows for a more cohesive security posture that leverages data from various sources for better decision-making. MDR services represent a significant advancement over traditional security measures by offering more adaptive, integrated, and responsive cybersecurity solutions. They are particularly well-suited to combating the sophisticated and rapidly evolving threats in today's digital landscape.

4 Must-Have Features in MDR Providers

MDR services not only offer comprehensive monitoring and response solutions but also integrate innovative technology, expert knowledge, and stringent compliance standards to protect against sophisticated cyber threats and attacks. Understanding the critical features of an effective MDR service is essential for businesses aiming to secure their digital assets and infrastructure effectively.

4.1 Technology Stack

A robust technology stack is fundamental to the effectiveness of an MDR provider. Key technologies that should be utilized include:

Advanced Machine Learning Models: These models are crucial for predicting and detecting new and evolving threats by analyzing patterns and anomalies that deviate from normal behavior.

Behavioral Analytics: This technology helps in understanding how users interact with systems and applications, enabling the detection of insider threats and compromised accounts.

Automated Response Systems: Automation in response mechanisms allows for the quick containment of threats, reducing the time from detection to response and minimizing potential damage. These technologies enable MDR services to offer dynamic and adaptive threat detection and response capabilities that are superior to traditional, rule-based security systems, which often fail to keep pace with the sophistication of modern cyber threats.

Types of systems monitored: MDRs should possess the capability to extend beyond IT and monitor Internet of Things (IOT) and Operational Technology (OT) as well. The latter two being especially important aspects for utilities, industrial, manufacturing and even transportation for cargo and maritime.

4.1.1 Expertise and Experience

The expertise and experience of an MDR provider are critical in delivering effective security solutions. An experienced MDR team offers:

Cross-Industry Knowledge: Providers with experience across various industries bring insights into specific security challenges and regulatory requirements, which can significantly enhance the threat detection and response strategies tailored for each client.

Threat Landscape Proficiency: Experienced providers are better equipped to manage the evolving threat landscape, as they continuously update their knowledge and skills to counteract new and emerging threats. Compared to in-house solutions, MDR providers typically have broader access to global threat intelligence networks and a more diverse experience, which enriches their understanding and response strategies to security incidents.

4.1.2 Service Level Agreements (SLAs)

SLAs are crucial in defining the expectations and responsibilities between MDR providers and their clients. Key components of an effective SLA include:

Response Times: These should be clearly defined to ensure that any detected threats are addressed swiftly to mitigate risks.

Resolution Metrics: SLAs should outline the metrics for measuring the resolution of incidents, including the steps involved in resolving several types of cyber threats.

Customer Support: Effective communication channels and support structures are vital for maintaining transparency and trust between the provider and the client. SLAs ensure that the MDR service meets the operational needs and security expectations of the client, providing a framework for accountability and performance.

4.1.3 Compliance and Certifications

Compliance with regulatory requirements and maintaining necessary security certifications are non-negotiable for credible MDR providers. Important standards and certifications a prospective MDR must have at least one of are:

ISO/IEC 27001: This international standard specifies the requirements for establishing, implementing, maintaining, and continually improving an information security management system (ISMS).

GDPR: The General Data Protection Regulation (GDPR) is a legal framework that sets guidelines for the collection and processing of personal information from individuals within the European Union (EU). Established by the EU, GDPR aims to give individuals control over their personal data and to simplify the regulatory environment for international business by unifying the regulation within the EU. It applies to all organizations operating within the EU and those outside the EU that offer goods or services to customers or businesses in the EU. Key elements include rights for individuals such as the right to access their data, the right to be forgotten, and the requirement for organizations to obtain explicit consent for data collection. Compliance is mandatory for organizations that manage EU residents' personal data.

PCI DSS: For organizations overseeing card payments, compliance with the Payment Card Industry Data Security Standard is essential to protect against data theft. These certifications not only demonstrate a provider's commitment to maintaining high security standards but also ensure that they can protect client data in accordance with international regulations.

SOC 2: (Service Organization Control 2) is a framework developed by the American Institute of CPAs (AICPA) for managing customer data in the cloud, ensuring its security, availability, processing integrity, confidentiality, and privacy. It applies to service providers and is essential for technology and cloud computing entities to demonstrate how their organizational controls comply with one or more of the five "trust service principles." These reports are crucial for demonstrating data management effectiveness to clients and auditors.

4.2 Customizability

Customizability is a critical feature that distinguishes superior providers from their competition. The ability to tailor services to the specific needs and risk profiles of each client underscores the importance of a personalized approach to cybersecurity. Customizability is essential in MDR services, especially given the unique characteristics of each organization.

4.2.1 Recognizing Individuality in Cybersecurity Needs

Every organization, even those within the same industry and utilizing similar technology stacks, possesses distinct operational practices, corporate cultures, and business strategies. These differences invariably influence their security vulnerabilities and the nature of the threats they are most likely to encounter. A one-size-fits-all approach, therefore, falls short of providing the nuanced protection modern businesses require.

Risk Profile Alignment: Effective MDR services start with a thorough understanding of a client's specific risk environment, including industry-specific threats, regulatory requirements, and unique business processes. This profiling is crucial as it dictates the protective measures that need to be prioritized.

Tailored Security Policies: Customizability allows MDR providers to design security policies and incident response plans that align closely with the client's operational requirements and risk tolerance. Custom policies ensure that security measures support, rather than inhibit, business operations.

4.2.2 The Benefits of Tailored MDR Services

Customizing an MDR solution enhances its effectiveness in several key areas:

Enhanced Threat Detection: By customizing the service, MDR providers can configure their detection tools to better recognize threats that are peculiar to the specific business or industry. This reduces the noise of false positives and sharpens the focus on genuine threats.

Targeted Response Actions: Custom responses are crafted based on the client's infrastructure and operational priorities, ensuring that incident response procedures are both swift and minimally disruptive to business operations.

Regulatory Compliance: Customizability ensures that compliance needs are met with precision, catering to specific industry regulations such as HIPAA for healthcare or PCI-DSS for finance, which can vary significantly from one organization to another.

4.2.3 Challenges and Considerations

While the benefits are significant, customizing MDR services also presents certain challenges:

Resource Intensity: Tailoring services can be resource intensive. It requires a deep dive into the client's systems and processes, which might involve considerable time and expertise.

Continuous Adjustment: As organizations evolve, so do their security needs. A customizable MDR service must be flexible enough to adapt to these changes, requiring ongoing engagement and iterative customization.

Cost Implications: Typically, the more customized the service, the higher the potential cost. Organizations must balance the level of customization with budget constraints while not compromising on critical security needs.

Customizability in MDR services is not just a value-added feature; it is a critical component of effective cybersecurity management. It acknowledges that while businesses may appear similar on the surface, underneath, their security needs can be vastly different. For executives and engineers looking to select an MDR provider, assessing the provider's ability to tailor their services to fit the unique contours of their organization is essential. This capability ensures that the security solutions provided are not only effective but also integrated seamlessly with the business's operational rhythms and strategic objectives.

The ability to tailor services to the specific needs and risk profiles of each client- and all clients are different! You are different than your closest peer who uses the same technology stack as you and is in the same business!

4.2.4 Integration Capabilities

Seamless integration with existing IT infrastructure and security solutions is an absolute must to gain maximum benefit from the MDR service provider. If you are using an MDR, you will already have or should have an Endpoint Detection and Response (EDR) solution. During operations, the EDR agent that resides on your end points, will feed alert and event information to the MDR service provider so they can digest and determine indicators of compromise (IOC). In most cases, an EDR solution from vendor A will be compatible with MDR vendor B – but there may be additional costs and compatibility issues involved so do check!

Additionally, some providers use MDR Agents which reside on system endpoints and feed alert and event information to the MDR service provider. These agents will need to be compatible with your existing EDR, Anti-Virus (AV) or other solution. This solution must at the very least "play well" with a prospective MDR vendor's solution. Please check the level of compatibility between your EDR, AV, others and the MDR agent.

Some MDRs receive alerts from system assets through an Application Programming Interface (API). This is helpful as it alleviates the need to use an agent which may cause compatibility issues with existing agents that reside on your system.

4.2.5 Scalability and Extensibility

The ability to scale services as your organization grows and extend its needs as the organization evolves means the MDR service provider will be required to accommodate this positive change. You may choose to add more cloud and data center assets and thus more endpoints, but you may also choose to add more assets to be monitored to include IOT, OT and infrastructure items such as Firewalls and Load balancers. In this case, the need for more extensible services would be required and an investigation into Extended Detection and Response (XDR) services would be warranted.

4.3 MDR versus XDR

Managed Detection and Response (MDR) and Extended Detection and Response (XDR) are both modern cybersecurity solutions designed to help organizations detect, analyze, and respond to threats. However, they differ in scope, capabilities, and integration.

4.3.1 MDR (Managed Detection and Response)

As we have already discussed, MDR focuses on providing organizations with outsourced security operations, including 24/7 monitoring, threat detection, and incident response services. It typically relies on a combination of technologies such as endpoint detection and response (EDR) and security information and event management (SIEM) systems, managed by a team of security experts. MDR services are designed to:

1. Detect and respond to threats on endpoints.
2. Offer security expertise and operational capabilities.
3. Provide continuous monitoring and management of security tools.

4.3.2 XDR (Extended Detection and Response)

XDR extends beyond endpoints to provide a more integrated approach to threat detection and response across multiple security layers, including email, network, server, cloud, and endpoints. XDR solutions aim to:

1. Consolidate data from multiple security products to improve threat detection and response.
2. Offer a unified platform that reduces complexity and enhances visibility across all environments.
3. Automate responses and correlate data across various security layers for faster resolution.

4.3.3 Key Differences

Scope and Integration: MDR services are typically more focused on endpoints and incorporate a variety of tools managed by the service provider. In contrast, XDR provides a more comprehensive integration of security tools across different layers of the IT environment, aiming to offer deeper visibility and more effective threat detection and response.

Automation and Response: XDR tends to emphasize more on automation and has capabilities to correlate data across different security domains to automate responses to detected threats. MDR may involve more manual processes, depending on the service provider.

Customization and Expertise: MDR services often include a significant level of human expertise and intervention, offering tailored threat hunting and response services. XDR solutions, while also potentially including service components, focus more on integrating and automating responses across a broader set of technologies.

In summary, while both MDR and XDR aim to enhance an organization's cybersecurity posture, the choice between them may depend on the specific needs, existing security infrastructure, and strategic goals of the organization. XDR offers a more integrated and automated approach suitable for environments looking for comprehensive visibility and fast response capabilities across all security layers, whereas MDR provides specialized expertise and outsourced security operations focused primarily on endpoints.

4.3.4 Reporting and Analytics

Comprehensive reporting tools and analytics for actionable insights and continuous improvement in security postures are essential for many purposes and people. For executives, comprehensive reporting, and analytics from an MDR service are crucial for making informed decisions that align with the organization's broader business objectives. These tools provide a high-level view of the security landscape, highlighting trends in attack vectors, the effectiveness of current security measures, and areas needing improvement.

With this data, executives can better understand their organization's risk profile, allocate resources more effectively, and justify cybersecurity investments. Moreover, clear, and concise reports help executives communicate security posture and needs to stakeholders, including board members who may not have a technical background.

In the context of digital forensics, detailed analytics and reporting are indispensable. When a security breach occurs, forensic investigators use data from MDR services to understand how the breach happened, which systems were compromised, and the data affected. This information is critical for conducting a thorough investigation, mitigating the damage, and preventing future incidents. Analytics help in identifying patterns that might indicate sophisticated cyber-attacks or persistent threats, enabling a more strategic response to incidents.

For cyber insurance providers, the data from MDR reporting and analytics can directly influence policy terms, premiums, and coverage limits. Insurers assess the risk profile of a company based on the security incidents reported, the response times, and the overall effectiveness of their cybersecurity measures. A company that consistently monitors its environment and responds effectively to incidents will be viewed as a lower risk, which can lead to more favorable insurance terms. Additionally, in the event of a claim, detailed reports can provide the necessary documentation to demonstrate compliance with policy conditions.

Analytics and reporting are fundamental to developing future cyber strategies. By continuously monitoring and analyzing threat data, organizations can identify emerging trends and adapt their cybersecurity strategies accordingly. This proactive approach helps in anticipating potential threats and mitigating them before they can cause harm. For instance, if reporting indicates an increase in phishing attacks targeting specific departments, a company can tailor its employee training programs and enhance its email security measures.

Overall, the integration of comprehensive reporting and analytics into MDR services offers actionable insights that drive continuous improvement in security postures. These capabilities not only support immediate tactical responses but also strategic planning and risk management, making them essential tools for executives, forensic teams, insurers, and anyone involved in shaping an organization's cyber defense strategy.

Choosing the right MDR provider involves a careful assessment of their technology stack, expertise, SLA specifics, compliance standards, and additional service features. By prioritizing these elements, organizations can significantly enhance their defensive capabilities against cyber threats, ensuring robust security in an increasingly digital world.

5 Evaluating and Selecting an MDR service

This chapter is designed to guide executives, non-technical and cyber-knowledgeable engineers through the process of evaluating and selecting an MDR provider, ensuring a fit that meets specific security needs and organizational goals.

5.1.1 Conducting a Security Needs Assessment

Before evaluating potential MDR providers, it is essential to conduct a comprehensive security needs assessment. This assessment should identify the organization's key digital assets, potential security threats, compliance requirements, and any existing cybersecurity measures. Understanding these elements will clarify what you need from an MDR service, ensuring that the chosen provider can meet your specific security requirements.

It is important to consider the various operational, strategic, and compliance-driven factors that influence the decision to procure an MDR service, below are several key reasons:

Managing Sensitive Customer Data: Organizations that collect, store, and process sensitive customer data (such as personal information, payment details, or health records) are prime targets for cyberattacks. MDR services offer advanced threat detection, monitoring, and response capabilities that can protect this data against breaches, helping organizations meet their data protection obligations and maintain customer trust.

Dependence on Network Reliability: Companies that operate networks crucial for customer operations, such as telecommunications providers, cloud service providers, and utilities, cannot afford significant downtime or disruptions caused by cyber incidents. MDR services provide continuous monitoring and rapid response to threats, helping to ensure network reliability and service continuity.

Providing Critical Services: Organizations that deliver essential services— whether in healthcare, financial, or government sectors—require robust cybersecurity to prevent disruptions that could have widespread repercussions. MDR can quickly identify and mitigate threats, thus safeguarding the integrity and availability of these critical services.

Hosting Sensitive Data: Entities that host sensitive data for other organizations using cloud service providers (CSPs) and data centers, are responsible for protecting that data against unauthorized access and cyber threats. MDR services can enhance their security posture and provide more confidence to win business by providing comprehensive monitoring, threat detection, and incident response, tailored to the specific security requirements of this hosted data. Know this when assessing an MDR- it is to also protect your customer's data.

Compliance with Regulatory Requirements: Many industries are subject to strict regulatory requirements regarding data protection and cybersecurity (e.g., GDPR, HIPAA, PCI-DSS). Non-compliance can result in hefty fines and reputational damage. MDR services help organizations comply with these regulations by ensuring that their cybersecurity measures are up to date and effective against emerging threats.

Lack of In-House Security Expertise: Small to medium-sized enterprises often lack the resources to maintain an in-house cybersecurity team. MDR services provide access to top-tier security experts and advanced technologies, offering a cost-effective solution for managing cyber risks without the need for extensive internal cybersecurity infrastructure.

Scalability and Flexibility: As organizations grow, so do their digital footprints and cybersecurity needs. MDR services are scalable and can adapt to the changing size and complexity of an organization, providing security measures that grow with the company.

Advanced Persistent Threats (APT): Facing sophisticated cyber threats like APTs requires advanced security measures. MDR services use innovative technologies and techniques to detect, analyze, and respond to these threats, providing a level of security that is hard to achieve with standard security solutions. Incorporating these considerations, an organization can better understand how MDR services play a critical role in enhancing their cybersecurity posture, ensuring operational continuity, and meeting compliance requirements. This proactive approach to cybersecurity enables organizations to focus on their core business functions while leaving security management to trusted experts.

5.1.2 Vendor Evaluation Criteria

Now that you have decided you need an MDR service, finding the most appropriate service provider will involve a lot of due diligence and research. When evaluating potential MDR providers, consider the following checklist to assess their suitability:

Technological Capabilities: Does the provider use advanced technologies like machine learning, behavioral analytics, and automated response systems? How do they integrate with existing systems? Assess the Detection Technologies to understand the range and sophistication of technologies used for threat detection, including endpoint detection and response (EDR), network traffic analysis, and advanced analytics capabilities. The MDR service should seamlessly integrate with your existing security tools and IT infrastructure. Compatibility with current systems minimizes disruptions and leverages your existing investments.

Consolidation of tools opportunities: Another advantageous aspect of MDR services that can help mitigate their cost is tools consolidation; the addition of an MDR service may mean that certain existing tools such as AV, EDR, Vulnerability Scanners and external scanning services may be replaceable through the MDR service that offers these or some of these services.

Reputation: What is the provider's standing in the industry? Look for awards, recognitions, and certifications that validate their credibility.

Client Testimonials: Seek feedback from current and former clients to gauge the effectiveness and reliability of the provider. How do they manage crisis situations?

Additional Services: Does the provider offer services beyond monitoring, such as incident response, crisis management, forensics, and post-attack recovery?

Cost Structures: Evaluate the pricing models. Are they transparent and predictable? Consider how they align with your budget and financial planning.

Response Capabilities: Understand the tools and processes in place for responding to detected threats, such as automated containment measures, the ability to execute remote remediation, and the speed of manual intervention when necessary.

5.1.3 Piloting and Decision Making

An MDR service should be piloted before the actual service is procured. Making an informed selection decision based on pilot outcomes involves analyzing the data collected, considering the ease of integration, effectiveness in threat detection and response, and feedback from the pilot team. The best practices for piloting or conducting a proof of concept with MDR services include:

Select a Pilot Scope: Define a specific segment of your network or a type of threat to focus on during the pilot to effectively evaluate the MDR's capabilities.

Measure Effectiveness: Establish clear metrics for success before starting the pilot, such as reduction in incident response time or improvement in detection rates.

Define Pilot success criteria: The success criteria must be first defined so that a decision can be made based on the outcome of the pilot.

Assess Compatibility: Evaluate how well the MDR service integrates with your existing cybersecurity infrastructure and practices.

Contract Negotiation: When negotiating contracts with MDR providers, consider the following strategies:

- **Pricing and Payments:** Negotiate terms that align with your financial workflow. Look for opportunities for volume discounts or bundled services which could offer cost savings.
- **Service Length:** Determine the appropriate contract length, often influenced by your assessment of the provider's adaptability to evolving cyber threats.
- **Extras:** Discuss potential for additional services, including regular security audits, customized reporting, or access to special consultancy.

Compliance and Certifications: Verify that the provider meets all relevant regulatory compliance standards and holds industry-recognized certifications.

Customer Support: Consider the provider's support structure and availability. Ensure they offer 24/7 support and have adequate resources to assist you when needed.

5.1.4 Cost Estimates: Data Vendors need to know.

When evaluating and pricing an MDR service, a vendor typically needs to gather specific technical information from the customer. This information helps the vendor accurately size, scale, and price their services according to the customer's unique environment and security needs. Here are the key technical items that a vendor would need to know:

5.1.5 Environment Size and Complexity

Number of Endpoints: This includes workstations, servers, and mobile devices.

Operating Systems: Windows, Mac, Linux, and many, various versions.

Network Architecture: Information on network topology, segmentation, and the number and types of network devices.

Cloud Usage: Details about cloud platforms in use (AWS, Azure, Google Cloud, etc.), including any managed and unmanaged cloud services.

5.1.6 Current Security Infrastructure

Existing Security Tools: Information about current antivirus, firewall, SIEM, and other security solutions in place.

Integration Capabilities: Details on existing security tools and systems that the MDR service will need to integrate with, including any APIs or custom integrations required.

5.1.7 Data Volume and Types

Traffic Volume: Average and peak data traffic volumes, which are crucial for assessing the scalability of the monitoring solutions.

Sensitive Data: Types of sensitive data managed and stored, and specific compliance requirements for this data (such as PCI-DSS, HIPAA, GDPR).

5.1.8 Regulatory and Compliance Requirements

Compliance Needs: Specific regulatory standards the organization needs to meet, which can affect the level of security monitoring and response required.

Audit Requirements: Any requirements for logging, report generation, and audit trails that need to be supported by the MDR service.

5.1.9 Operational Requirements and Expectations

Service Level Agreements (SLAs): Desired response times for threat detection and incident response.

Threat Protection Levels: Specific threats the organization is most concerned about, which can influence the focus and sophistication of the MDR service.

5.1.10 Budget Constraints

Budget Information: Understanding of the financial constraints or targets that the organization aims to adhere to, which can dictate the scope and scale of the MDR services offered.

5.1.11 Future Growth Plans

Scalability Requirements: Information about expected growth in network size, data volume, or global expansion that may affect future security needs.

Collecting and analyzing these details allows the MDR vendor to tailor their service offering to effectively meet the customer's security requirements, operational dynamics, and financial constraints. This alignment is critical for ensuring that the MDR service not only fits the current security posture but also scales with the organization as it evolves.

5.1.12 The Down-Select Process

The down-select process involves narrowing down potential providers through successive rounds of evaluation based on the criteria outlined above. A project manager can be instrumental in this process by coordinating evaluation activities, consulting with stakeholders, and ensuring that all requirements are comprehensively assessed.

By following these guidelines, executives and engineers can make a well-informed decision when selecting an MDR service, enhancing their organization's cybersecurity posture and resilience against threats.

6 Integration & Implementation Challenges

Integrating and implementing MDR services into an existing cybersecurity infrastructure presents a range of technical and operational challenges. Addressing these challenges effectively is crucial for maximizing the benefits of MDR services. This chapter will explore common integration issues, provide mitigation strategies, and discuss best practices for ensuring smooth integration and ongoing operations.

6.1 Integration Issues- Common Technical Challenges

Integrating Managed Detection and Response (MDR) services into an organization's existing security infrastructure can be a complex task fraught with technical and operational challenges. However, with the right strategies and best practices, these challenges can be effectively managed to ensure a seamless integration and optimal functioning of the MDR service.

6.1.1 Compatibility with Existing Systems:

MDR tools are often built with the latest technologies that may not mesh well with older, legacy systems that are prevalent in many organizations. These legacy systems may lack the necessary APIs or support for modern protocols, hindering effective integration. This mismatch can lead to gaps in data collection and analysis capabilities, potentially leaving parts of the network inadequately protected.

6.1.2 Mitigation Strategies

Interoperability Assessments: Before integration, conduct a thorough assessment of the current IT infrastructure to identify potential compatibility issues and plan accordingly. If necessary, conduct a threat modeling exercise or at the very least, go through some what-if scenarios, engaging the vendor who will possess a quantity of experience from integrating their system with many different customers.

System Assessment and Upgrades: Conduct a comprehensive assessment of the existing IT infrastructure to identify compatibility issues. This assessment can guide necessary upgrades or replacements that facilitate better integration with modern MDR solutions.

Custom Adapters: Develop custom adapters or middleware that can serve as a bridge between legacy systems and new MDR tools, ensuring that data flows seamlessly across all parts of the IT environment.

6.2 Complexity in Configuration

Setting up an MDR service requires a detailed understanding of the organization's network architecture, data flows, and security policies. MDR systems must be finely tuned to align with specific organizational needs, which can be technically demanding and resource intensive. Without proper configuration, the effectiveness of the MDR service might be compromised, failing to detect threats accurately or generating excessive false positives.

6.2.1 Mitigation Strategies

Involve IT staff early in the planning stage to align the MDR configuration with existing security policies and procedures.

Leverage the expertise of MDR vendors for initial setup and configuration, ensuring that all system components are correctly aligned and functional.

Implement continuous training programs for IT staff to manage and adjust MDR settings as organizational needs evolve.

6.3 Data Overload

Integrating MDR services often involves aggregating data from various sources, including network traffic, logs, endpoint sensors, and more. This integration can lead to a tremendous volume of data, which can overwhelm systems and analysts alike, complicating the task of distinguishing genuine threats from benign anomalies or false positives.

6.3.1 Mitigation Strategies

Use data aggregation and correlation tools: to filter out irrelevant data and highlight potential threats.

Advanced Filtering Techniques: Implement advanced data filtering and aggregation techniques to manage data overload and improve results.

Apply advanced analytics and machine learning: to enhance the accuracy of threat detection and reduce noise.

Continuously refine data inputs and tuning parameters: to balance the quantity and quality of security alerts, continuously tuning the alert system to reduce false positives and ensure that security teams can focus on genuine threats.

Vendor Support: Choose MDR providers who offer robust support for integration issues and are willing to work closely with your IT team to resolve compatibility problems and improve the quality of threat data.

Training and Development: Invest in training for current IT staff to fill any skill gaps and ensure they are equipped to manage the MDR service.

Structured Change Management: Apply structured change management practices to ease the integration process and foster acceptance among staff.

6.4 Operational Challenges

Skill Gaps: MDR services require a combination of advanced cybersecurity, analytical, and incident response skills that may not be present in the existing IT staff. This gap can hinder the effective implementation and ongoing management of MDR services, impacting the organization's ability to swiftly identify and mitigate threats.

Change Management: The integration of MDR services can disrupt existing workflows, leading to resistance from staff who are accustomed to traditional processes. This resistance can slow down or undermine the integration process, affecting the effectiveness of the new system.

Early and continuous engagement with all stakeholders, including IT staff, management, and end-users, is crucial. This involves clear communication about the benefits of MDR, how it will affect their daily work, and the role they play in its success. Incremental Implementation of MDR services in phases can help the organization adjust more gradually. This phased approach allows staff to become familiar with the new system slowly, reducing resistance and increasing acceptance.

Alert Fatigue: High volumes of alerts, many of which may be false positives, can lead to alert fatigue among security personnel.

6.4.1 Mitigation Strategies

Training and Development: Invest in training for current IT staff to fill any skill gaps and ensure they are equipped to manage the MDR service.

Structured Change Management: Apply structured change management practices to ease the integration process and foster acceptance among staff.

Tuning Alert Systems: Continuously tune the alert system to reduce false positives and ensure that security teams can focus on genuine threats.

Feedback Loops: Establish effective feedback mechanisms to capture the concerns and suggestions of the staff affected by the new system. This can inform ongoing improvements and increase staff buy-in.

Pilot Testing: Conduct pilot testing of the MDR system in a controlled environment to identify any issues before full-scale deployment.

Incremental Integration: Roll out the MDR service incrementally to manage the complexity of integration and minimize disruptions to existing operations.

6.5 Best Practices for MDR Integration and Operations

6.5.1 Integrating MDR into Incident Response Plans (IRP):

It is crucial that MDR services are woven into existing Incident Response Plans to create a unified response mechanism. The MDR service will provide the data they have gathered and their conclusions to date for the on-going incident. It is vital they are now incorporated in the IRP as they will, if anything, be a main driver and contributor to the response to drive it to resolution.

6.5.2 Best Practices:

Update IRP protocols to include MDR processes, ensuring that roles, responsibilities, and procedures are clear and actionable. Share the IRP with the MDR provider to obtain input, guidance and any changes that are required to enable the MDR provider to deliver the best service.

Conduct regular IRP drills that include MDR scenarios to evaluate the system's effectiveness and the team's readiness. Develop Tabletop Exercise scenarios and run through a drill that will involve the MDR to the best possible degree.

Use insights gained from MDR actions to continually enhance IRP strategies, making them more responsive to detected threats.

7 Justification of MDR Investments

When organizations invest in Managed Detection and Response (MDR) services, they are not only acquiring a defense mechanism but also making a strategic investment in their overall cybersecurity posture. The justification of this investment hinges significantly on the ability of the MDR service to provide high-quality alerts that translate into actionable intelligence and measurable outcomes. Below is a detailed look at how businesses can ensure the volume and quality of alerts justify the investment in MDR services.

7.1 Understanding the Value of Quality Alerts

Quality Over Quantity: It is essential for MDR services to focus on the quality of alerts rather than the sheer volume. High-quality alerts are those that accurately identify real threats and provide sufficient detail to enable rapid response. This reduces the time and resources spent investigating false positives.

Advanced Analytics: Employing advanced analytics helps in distinguishing between genuine threats and noise. This involves using sophisticated algorithms to analyze patterns and behaviors in network traffic.

Contextual Information: Alerts that include contextual information about the threat can drastically improve response times and effectiveness. Context helps in understanding the nature of the threat, its potential impact, and the best course of action to mitigate it.

7.2 Measuring the Effectiveness of MDR Alerts:

Metrics for Measurement: To justify the investment, organizations need to develop clear metrics that can measure the effectiveness of MDR alerts and if they were warranted.

Detection Rate: How often the MDR service successfully detects real threats compared to missed incidents.

False Positive Rate: An essential metric that measures the accuracy of the alerts. A high rate of false positives can drain resources and divert attention from genuine threats.

Response Time: The speed with which the security team can respond to an alert. Faster response times can mitigate potential damage and are indicative of the alert's actionable quality.

ROI Calculation: Return on Investment (ROI) in cybersecurity can be challenging to calculate but is crucial for justifying MDR expenditures. This can be approached by assessing the costs of breaches that were prevented owing to timely MDR alerts versus the cost of the MDR service.

Cost Avoidance: Calculate the potential losses avoided through effective threat detection and response. This includes direct costs like downtime and data loss, and indirect costs like reputational damage.

Operational Efficiency: MDR services can streamline cybersecurity operations by automating routine tasks and consolidating incident data, which leads to improved operational efficiency.

7.2.1 Leveraging MDR Data for Continuous Improvement

Feedback Loops: Creating feedback loops where the response to alerts is analyzed to refine the detection mechanisms continuously.

Adjusting Thresholds: Based on feedback, adjusting the sensitivity of alert systems to balance between catching real threats and generating false positives.

Tailored Threat Intelligence: Using the data collected from past alerts to tailor the threat intelligence to the specific environment of the organization. This can help in anticipating and preparing for potential future threats more effectively.

Reporting and Communication: Regular reporting on MDR performance to stakeholders is crucial. These reports should highlight success stories and demonstrate how MDR contributes to maintaining security posture.

Case Studies: Document specific instances where the MDR service successfully detected and mitigated threats. This can provide concrete examples of the service's value.

Strategic Reviews: Conduct periodic reviews of MDR strategy to ensure it aligns with the evolving threat landscape and business objectives.

Justifying the investment in MDR services requires a focus on quality, effectiveness, and continuous improvement of alert mechanisms. By measuring the right metrics, calculating ROI, and leveraging data for improvements, organizations can ensure that their investment in MDR services delivers substantial value in maintaining robust cybersecurity defenses.

7.3 Ongoing Operations

Regular Reviews and Adjustments: Regularly review and adjust the configurations of the MDR system to align with evolving security needs and threat landscapes.

Integration with Incident Response Plans (IRP): Ensure that MDR services are fully integrated into the organization's IRP to enhance the overall response to incidents.

Balancing Alerts and Events: Fine-tune the MDR settings to balance the number of alerts and events generated. This helps justify the MDR's value to the organization while avoiding overwhelming security personnel.

7.4 Ensuring Justification for MDR

The integration and implementation of MDR services involves navigating several technical and operational challenges. By understanding these challenges and applying effective mitigation strategies and best practices, organizations can ensure a successful integration of MDR services, enhancing their cybersecurity posture while maintaining operational efficiency.

This proactive approach not only addresses immediate security needs but also positions the organization well for future threats. Establish clear metrics to measure the performance of the MDR service, including detection rates, response times, and incident handling efficiency. Provide regular and comprehensive reports to stakeholders to demonstrate the effectiveness and value of the MDR service.

8 Future Trends and Innovations in MDR

As our world and IT evolves, so too does the nature of cyber threats, demanding ever more advanced defenses. MDR services are at the forefront of adopting emerging technologies like artificial intelligence (AI) and blockchain to enhance cybersecurity measures. This chapter explores the potential impacts of these technologies on MDR services, focusing on the development of predictive security models and the tailoring of services to meet industry-specific needs.

8.1 Artificial Intelligence in MDR Services

Enhancing Detection and Response: AI is revolutionizing MDR services by enhancing both threat detection and response capabilities. Machine learning algorithms can analyze vast datasets rapidly, identifying patterns and anomalies that may indicate a cyber threat. This capability not only speeds up the response times but also increases accuracy, reducing the rate of false positives.

Predictive Security: AI's predictive capabilities are one of its most transformative aspects in cybersecurity. By using historical data, AI models can predict and identify potential threats before they manifest, allowing preemptive action to be taken. This shift from reactive to proactive security is a significant advancement towards more robust cybersecurity frameworks.

Automated Response: AI enables automated responses to security incidents, which is crucial for containing threats quickly. For instance, if a potential threat is detected, AI systems can automatically isolate affected systems or cut off certain network accesses, containing the threat until human responders can take over.

8.2 Blockchain's Role in MDR Services

Enhancing Integrity and Traceability: Blockchain technology can significantly enhance the integrity and traceability of transactions within an organization's network. By logging transactions on a decentralized and immutable ledger, blockchain provides a verifiable and tamper-proof record-keeping system.

Securing Decentralized Data: In MDR, blockchain can secure logs and data critical for forensic analysis, ensuring that they have not been altered post-incident. This capability is crucial for maintaining the integrity of evidence in the aftermath of a cybersecurity breach.

Smart Contracts for Automated Enforcement: Blockchain can also be utilized to deploy smart contracts that automatically enforce security policies when certain conditions are met, further reducing the time to respond to incidents and ensuring consistent application of security protocols.

8.3 Industry-Specific Evolution of MDR Services

Tailored Security Solutions: As different industries face unique threats based on their environment and the nature of their data, MDR services are increasingly becoming specialized to cater to these specific needs.

Healthcare: For instance, MDR services in healthcare focus on protecting patient information complying with regulations such as HIPAA. Advanced AI models are used to monitor and protect patient data from ransomware attacks and data breaches.

Financial Services: In the financial sector, MDR services are tailored to prevent financial fraud and protect against breaches involving sensitive financial information. Blockchain is particularly impactful in this sector for ensuring the integrity of transaction records.

Manufacturing: For manufacturing, where the integration of IOT and OT devices is prevalent, MDR services focus on securing these devices and the data they generate, which are often susceptible to unique threats like industrial espionage and sabotage.

8.4 What to Expect from Vendors and Internal Teams

Continuous Innovation: Executives and engineers should expect MDR vendors to continually innovate and integrate modern technologies like AI and blockchain into their services. This involves not just adopting these technologies but also developing expertise to effectively implement and manage them.

Collaboration and Customization: MDR services should be seen as a collaborative and customizable effort tailored to the specific needs of the business. Vendors must collaborate closely with internal teams to understand their unique environments and tailor their offerings accordingly.

Education and Training: It is crucial for internal teams to receive ongoing education and training on the latest technologies and threats. This ensures that they can effectively collaborate with MDR providers and respond appropriately to the insights provided by these advanced systems.

The integration of AI and blockchain into MDR services represents a significant leap forward in the fight against cybercrime. These technologies enable more predictive, responsive, and tailored cybersecurity solutions, providing businesses with the tools they need to defend against increasingly sophisticated threats. As these technologies continue to evolve, so will the capabilities of MDR services, promising a future where cyber defenses are not only reactive but predictive, intelligent, and finely tuned to the specific needs of each industry.

9   Compliance with Cyber Frameworks

Using an MDR service can help your organization meet specific controls across several regulatory and security frameworks, including SOC 2 Type 2, NIST CSF (Cybersecurity Framework), and ISO 27001. By incorporating an MDR service, your organization can address these specific controls more effectively, ensuring a robust monitoring, detection, and response system is in place. Each control mentioned aligns with the capabilities of MDR to enhance your security posture and meet compliance requirements comprehensively.

During an audit, documenting how the MDR service contributes to these controls is crucial. Ensure to keep detailed records and reports that demonstrate the MDR's effectiveness in meeting these standards. Here is a breakdown of how MDR services typically align with these standards:

9.1   SOC 2 Type 2 Controls

SOC 2 focuses on the Trust Service Criteria of Security, Availability, Processing Integrity, Confidentiality, and Privacy. Key controls that an MDR service supports typically relate to the Security and Availability criteria:

CC6.1 Control Activities: The entity uses detection and monitoring procedures to identify (detect) changes to configurations that result in the introduction of new vulnerabilities.

CC6.8 Detection and Monitoring: The entity monitors system components and the operation of those components for anomalies indicative of malicious acts, natural disasters, and errors affecting the entity's ability to meet its objectives.

9.2 NIST Cybersecurity Framework (CSF)

The NIST CSF has several relevant categories where specific controls can be addressed by MDR services:

DE.CM-1 Detection Processes: Network and physical activities are monitored to detect potential cybersecurity events.

DE.CM-7: Monitoring for Information Security Events: The information system and assets are monitored to identify cybersecurity events and verify the effectiveness of protective measures.

PR.PT-1: Protective Technology: Audit/log records are determined, documented, implemented, and reviewed in accordance with policy.

9.3 ISO 27001 Security Controls

ISO 27001 outlines a comprehensive set of information security control objectives and controls. Relevant ones include:

A.12.4.1 Event Logging: Logs user activities, exceptions, faults, and information security events are produced and kept for an agreed period to assist in future investigations and access control monitoring.

A.16.1.1 Management of Info Security Incidents and Improvements: Consistently apply the information security incident management process.

A.12.6.1 Management of Technical Vulnerabilities: Information about technical vulnerabilities of information systems being used is obtained in a timely fashion, the organization's exposure to such vulnerabilities evaluated, and appropriate measures taken to address the associated risk.

10 MDR and XDR Providers

The list of global MDR and XDR providers is exceptionally long. Below is a selection of some of the many providers to choose from:

10.1 MDR Providers

CrowdStrike - Known for its Falcon platform, CrowdStrike offers comprehensive endpoint protection along with threat intelligence and incident response services.

Rapid7 - Provides MDR services with a focus on using advanced analytics to detect and respond to threats across various vectors.

Secureworks - Offers an MDR solution that blends advanced analytics, threat intelligence, and human expertise to provide enhanced security operations.

Arctic Wolf - Known for its security operations solutions, Arctic Wolf offers tailored MDR services that focus on providing personalized threat detection and response.

Alert Logic - Specializes in cloud-based MDR solutions, providing full-stack security monitoring and response capabilities.

LTI Global – a service provider dedicated to IOT and OT services specializing in the utilities and marine verticals.

10.2 XDR Providers

Palo Alto Networks - Their Cortex XDR platform integrates network, endpoint, and cloud data to prevent sophisticated attacks.

Trend Micro - Provides an XDR solution that correlates data across email, endpoints, servers, cloud workloads, and networks to improve threat detection.

Sophos - Offers an XDR solution that allows organizations to investigate threats using rich data and enhances their overall security operations.

McAfee - Known for a wide range of security solutions, McAfee offers an XDR platform that combines analytics and machine learning to improve threat detection and response.

Fortinet - Their FortiXDR is an automated XDR solution designed to reduce complexity in the threat response by using artificial intelligence to analyze alerts.

These companies are recognized for their advanced capabilities in handling cybersecurity threats, leveraging a combination of technology and human expertise to protect organizations. When choosing an MDR or XDR provider, it is essential to consider your specific security needs, the scale of your operations, and the strengths of each provider. Below is a longer list, but it does not cover the entire global list!

1. Sophos
2. SentinelOne Vigilance Respond
3. Alert
4. Arctic Wolf
5. ReliaQuest
6. Secureworks Taegis ManagedXDR
7. Red Canary
8. Cybereason
9. Expel
10. Critical Start
11. eSentire
12. Deepwatch
13. SISA ProACT
14. Binary Defense
15. Ontinue ION MXDR
16. CYBEROO
17. Kroll Responder
18. Mandiant
19. Unit 42 MDR Service
20. Trustwave
21. ESET

11 Glossary

For a great Cyber Glossary, please go here: https://www.sans.org/security-resources/glossary-of-terms/ but here are some typical Cyber terms.

- **Access Control**: The process of granting or denying specific requests to obtain and use information and related information processing services.
- **Adware**: Software designed to force pre-chosen ads to display on your system.
- **Advanced Persistent Threat (APT)**: A prolonged and targeted cyberattack in which an intruder gains access to a network and remains undetected for an extended period.
- **Antivirus Software**: A program that monitors a computer or network to identify all major types of malware and prevent or contain malware incidents.
- **Botnet**: A network of private computers infected with malicious software and controlled as a group without the owners' knowledge, e.g., to transmit spam.
- **Blockchain**: A system in which a record of transactions made in cryptocurrency is maintained across several computers that are linked in a peer-to-peer network.
- **Brute Force Attack**: A trial and error method used by application programs to decode encrypted data such as passwords or Data Encryption Standard (DES) keys, through exhaustive effort rather than employing intellectual strategies.
- **Cloud Security**: A collection of procedures and technology designed to address external and internal threats to business security.
- **Cybersecurity**: The protection of internet-connected systems, including hardware, software, and data, from cyberattacks.
- **Cryptocurrency**: A digital or virtual currency that uses cryptography for security.
- **Cross-Site Scripting (XSS)**: A type of security vulnerability typically found in web applications. XSS enables attackers to inject client-side scripts into web pages viewed by other users.
- **DDoS (Distributed Denial of Service)**: An attack that shuts down a machine or network, making it inaccessible to its intended users.
- **Data Breach**: A security incident in which information is accessed without authorization.
- **Data Encryption**: The process of converting information or data into a code, especially to prevent unauthorized access.
- **Digital Signature**: A mathematical scheme for verifying the authenticity of digital messages or documents.
- **Encryption**: The process of converting data or information into code to prevent unauthorized access.
- **Endpoint Security**: The process of securing the data and workflows associated with the individual devices that connect to your network.
- **Ethical Hacking**: Legally breaking into computers and devices to evaluate an organization's defenses.
- **Firewall**: A network security device that monitors incoming and outgoing network traffic and permits or blocks data packets based on a set of security rules.

- **Forensics**: The application of scientific knowledge to the investigation of crimes.
- **Gateway**: A network point that acts as an entrance to another network.
- **Hacker**: A person who uses computers to gain unauthorized access to data.
- **HTTP (Hypertext Transfer Protocol)**: The protocol used for transmitting web pages over the Internet.
- **IP Address**: A unique string of numbers separated by periods that identifies each computer using the Internet Protocol to communicate over a network.
- **Intrusion Detection System (IDS)**: A device or software application that monitors a network or systems for malicious activity or policy violations.
- **JavaScript**: A scripting language used to create and control dynamic website content.
- **Keylogger**: A program that records the real-time activity of a computer user including the keys they press.
- **LAN (Local Area Network)**: A network that connects computers within a limited area such as a residence, school, or office building.
- **Malware**: Software that is intended to damage or disable computers and computer systems.
- **MDR (Managed Detection and Response)**: A service that provides organizations with threat hunting, monitoring, and response solutions through a turnkey approach. MDR providers use a combination of advanced technologies and human expertise to monitor, assess, and defend enterprises from cyber threats.
- **Network Security**: The practice of preventing and protecting against unauthorized intrusion into corporate networks.
- **OAuth**: An open standard for access delegation, commonly used as a way for Internet users to grant websites or applications access to their information on other websites but without giving them the passwords.
- **Phishing**: A method of trying to gather personal information using deceptive e-mails and websites.
- **Proxy Server**: A server that acts as an intermediary for requests from clients seeking resources from other servers.
- **Quantum Cryptography**: The use of the principles of quantum mechanics to enhance the security of data transmission.
- **Ransomware**: Malware that encrypts a user's files and demands payment in exchange for the key to decrypt the information.
- **Rootkit**: A set of software tools that enable an unauthorized user to gain control of a computer system without being detected.
- **Security Information and Event Management (SIEM)**: Software that provides real-time analysis of security alerts generated by applications and network hardware.
- **Social Engineering**: The use of deception to manipulate individuals into divulging confidential or personal information that may be used for fraudulent purposes.
- **SSL (Secure Sockets Layer)**: A standard security technology for establishing an encrypted link between a server and a client.
- **Trojan Horse**: A type of malware that is often disguised as legitimate software.

- **Two-Factor Authentication (2FA)**: A security process in which the user provides two different authentication factors to verify themselves.
- **URL Filtering**: The practice of blocking access to certain websites or webpages based on the URL.
- **Virus**: A type of malicious software program that, when executed, replicates by reproducing itself or infecting other programs by modifying them.
- **Virtual Private Network (VPN)**: A network that is constructed using public wires — usually the Internet — to connect to a private network, such as a company's internal network.
- **Worm**: A standalone malware computer program that replicates itself to spread to other computers.
- **XSS (Cross-Site Scripting)**: A security vulnerability typically found in web applications which allows attackers to inject client-side scripts into web pages viewed by other users.
- **YARA**: A tool aimed at (but not limited to) helping malware researchers to identify and classify malware samples.
- **Zero-Day Attack**: An attack that exploits a previously unknown security vulnerability, meaning the software vendor has not had time to release a fix.

www.ingramcontent.com/pod-product-compliance
Lightning Source LLC
LaVergne TN
LVHW081532050326
832903LV00025B/1764